Taste

Written by Mandy Suhr
and
Illustrated by Mike Gordon

Wayland

The Senses

Hearing
Sight
Smell
Taste
Touch

First publshed in 1993 by
Wayland (Publishers) Ltd.
61 Western Road, Hove
East Sussex, BN3 1JD

© Copyright Wayland (Publishers) Limited
Series Editor: Mandy Suhr
Consultants: Jane Battell and Richard Killick

British Library Cataloguing in Publication Data

Suhr , Mandy
 Taste - (Senses series)
 I. Title II. Gordon , Mike III. Series
 612.8

ISBN 0-7502-0659-4

Typeset by Wayland (Publishers) Ltd.
Printed and bound in Belgium by Casterman S.A.

Contents

Look inside this shop. All these foods have a different taste.

What do you think
they might taste like?

5

Some things taste sweet.

Some things taste salty.

Some things taste sour...

or bitter.

Some foods taste really good when they are tasted together!

You should never taste something if you are not sure what it is. It may be poisonous.

Even some things that animals or birds eat can be poisonous for people.

We taste things using our tongues.

Inside your tongue are lots of tiny taste detectors. These are called taste buds.

When you put food into your mouth, the taste buds on different parts of your tongue detect different kinds of tastes.

These taste buds detect bitter tastes...

these detect salty tastes...

these detect sweet tastes...

these detect sour tastes.

17

Your tongue can also tell you
whether foods are cold...

or hot...

and what they feel like.

All your senses work together, but smell and taste are special partners. When you smell something, it helps you to guess what the taste will be like.

If you have a cold and your nose is blocked, then often you can't smell or taste things very well.

Most animals also have a sense of taste. Some have taste buds.

But many animals have other ways of tasting things. Flies can even taste through their feet!

Some animals are very fussy
about the taste of their food...

but others don't seem to
mind at all!

What are your favourite tastes?

Ask an adult to help you and your friends play this taste game. Can your friends guess what each food is just by tasting it?

Now hold your nose. Can you still guess what each food is by tasting it?

Notes for adults

'The Senses' is a series of first information books especially designed for the early stages of reading. Each book has a simple, factual text and amusing illustrations, combining reading for pleasure with fact-finding.

The content of the book addresses the requirements of the National Curriculum for Science, Key Stage One. The series takes a closer look at the human body, explaining very simply how we use each of our senses to learn about the world around us. This book explores the sense of taste.

The books are equally suitable for use at home or at school. Below are some suggestions for extension activities to complement the learning in this book.

1. Design a taste game using the one in this book as an example. This activity promotes collaborative learning when carried out in small groups.It encourages dicussion and hypothesising, both important language skills. Children can also be encouraged to develop a scoring system to incorporate practise of numerical skills.

2. Practise grouping and ordering skills. Foods can be arranged according to their taste and then ordered within their group,ie., foods which taste most to least sweet. This involves designing experiments, discussion, using mathematical sets and provides a variety of opportunities for recording of results eg. graphs, tables, setting up and using data bases.

3. Language work can involve brainstorming words to describe foods and making up new words to describe different tastes. These and other words can be used to create onomatopoeic poetry. Children can also make menus and cookery cards for their favourite foods.

4. Food technology. Create a tasty meal, looking at the importance of a balanced diet. Children should also consider what is necessary when setting up an environment for food production. They can design menus and advertising for the food they are producing.

Books to read

Experiment with Senses by Monica Byles (Toucan, 1992)

The Senses by K. Davies and W. Oldfield (Wayland, 1991)

Taste by Wayne Jackman (Wayland, 1989)

Tasting by Henry Pluckrose (Watts, 1990)

When I eat by Mandy Suhr (Wayland, 1991)

My Science Book of Senses by N. Ardley (Dorling Kindersley, 1992)